NBR TODAY PROTECTION OF WOMEN FROM DOMESTIC VIOLENCE READY RECKONER

FCS NAVEEN BHATNAGAR

ISBN 978-1-63832-676-2

My Beloved Parents (Late) Er. K.P. Bhatnagar & Savita Bhatnagar are a
constant inspiration. All my works are dedicated to their Lotus Feet.

Contents

FOREWORD

FCS Naveen Bhatnagar
    Celebrated Author Globally

OM Sai Ram... Friends, Readers, Dear Students, NBR Today is Your Friend Next-Door.

Blessed to be Mentored by IIM Founders; Govt/Political dispensation and more. Privileged to have Advised Leading Film, Sports Celebrities World-over. From Mahi, Choti Sardarni, Neil John Taylor, Craig Mc Dermott....never ending company, ever-since childhood.

Strong acumen to learning, mentoring helped me make 'SMILE' with a purpose. Equally, blessed over 1,000 Lovely Students in Multi-faceted areas such as Law, Economics, Costing, Accountancy, Financial Management. My Authored Book's (presently 17 Book's, increasing @ 15 Days) seeks your overwhelming support, blessing. **In 07 Hrs Master any Subject.**

PREFACE

NBR Today® provides Bare Act/s, Subject/s of interest for Professionals; Students pursuing Competitive Exams, Professional Courses in form of Ready Reckoner/ Digest/ Guide. NBR Today® is focussed to enhance, support common man's Knowledge, Understanding & gained reasonable recognition amongst Students, Academicians, Professional's, Government. It is easy to read, understand & grasp & for those matters connected therewith or incidental thereto.

Please note with caution that no work is complete, unless supplemented with practice, books, notes, guidance from Teachers, Elders & above all – Parents Love & Respect.

All possible precaution & care has been taken in this material to avoid mistakes & omissions etc. for which the Author/Editor, publisher and /or the sellers are not in any way responsible. All disputes are subject to Delhi Courts. Maximum liability is limited to return amount paid by concerned purchaser/ reader.

ACKNOWLEDGEMENTS

Author acknowledges invaluable contribution of his **Wife & Daughter**who took considerable pains in the development & review of the title, manuscript. Also, professional colleagues, relatives who took pains & reworked & updated this material to meet, suit requirement of the Reader's.

We will be failing in our duty if we do not acknowledge the contribution of *Amazon, Flipkart, Notion Press, etc.* who helped in publishing & in bringing out this material, publication.

In end, each one of our students is a precious 'Gem' – generation next, entering the new arena, aspiring to seek higher education, especially as professionals, opening new frontiers, all this to unravel "Excellence" as they move up in the higher echelons as Academician, Corporate Ladder, successful Entrepreneur, Home-makers. For sure, your rich idea's, honest feedback will certainly help improve, enrich to serve in a better way.

PROLOGUE

NBR Today® is focussed to enhance, support common man's Legal Knowledge, Understanding & gained reasonable recognition amongst Students, Academicians, Professional's, Government. A number of Voluminous yet Complex Laws affect every Indian's daily chores, which are avidly considered & addressed/answered in NBR Today®. Untiring Journey towards Excellence in the field of Law is what least I get inspired & NBR Today® is one such effort. I continue to do a lot of work for Professional enrichment & Prime importance.

I

Protection of Women from Domestic Violence Act, 2005

CHAPTER I: PRELIMINARY

1. Short title, extent & commencement: Extends to whole of India.

2. Definitions:

(a) "Agg. P" is woman in DR with Resp. & allege subject to DV by Resp.

(b) "Child" below 18 Yrs & include adopted, step/foster child.

(e) "DIR" report in PF on complaint of DV receipt from Agg. P.

(f) "DR" relation between 2 persons live/have, at any point of time, lived together in shared household, related by consanguinity, marriage or relation in nature of marriage, adoption/family members living together as joint family.

(i) "Mag." 1st Class JM/MM, exercise Jur. under Cr.PC in area where Agg.P reside temporary/otherwise/Resp. reside/DV alleged taken place.

(j) "MF" facility as CG notify be MF for PTA.

(k) "Monetary Relief" compensation which Mag. order Resp. pay to Agg. P any stage during Appl. hear seeking any relief UTA, to meet expenses incurred & loss suffered by Agg. P as a result of D.

(q) "Resp." adult male been in DR with Agg. P & against whom Agg. P sought relief UTA. Aggrieved wife/female living in relationship in nature of marriage may also file complaint against a relative of husband/male partner.

(s) "Shared Household" household where Agg. P live/any stage lived in DR with Resp. & include where own/tenant/jointly/singly have any right, title, etc. & include household joint family belong of which Resp. is member, irrespective of where Resp./Agg. P has any right, title etc. in shared household.

(t) "SH" CG notify as shelter home for PTA.

CHAPTER II: DOMESTIC VIOLENCE

3. DV Defined: any act, omission, etc. Resp. harms/injures Agg. P life, etc. whether mental/physical/tends to do so & include physical/sexual abuse/ verbal & emotional & economic abuse (OR) harass, harms, etc. her to meet any unlawful demand for dowry, etc. (OR) threaten her/any person related by any of herein conduct (OR) otherwise injures/causes harm to her. "physical abuse" means act/conduct cause bodily pain, harm, etc. & includes assault, criminal intimidate, etc.; "sexual abuse" include abuse, humiliate, etc. otherwise violate dignity of woman; "verbal & emotional abuse" include insults, ridicule, etc. especially not have child/male child & repeated threats to cause physical pain to any person in whom she is interested; "economic abuse" include deprive all/ any economic/ financial resources to which she is entitled under any law, etc. not limited to house hold necessities for she & her children, if any, stridhan, property, jointly/separately owned by her, payment of rental related to shared house hold & maintenance; dispose household effects, assets alienate in which her interest by virtue of DR/ reasonably required by her/children/stridhan/ property jointly/separately held by her & prohibit/restrict to facility, etc. which she is entitle to use/ enjoy by virtue of DR include access to shared household. To determine omission, etc. by Resp. constitute "DV" overall facts & circumstances of case take.

CHAPTER III: POWERS & DUTIES OF PROTECTION OFFICERS, SERVICE PROVIDERS, ETC.

4. Inform Prt. O: Any person believe DV been/being/likely commit, inform Prt. O concern & not liable, civil/criminal act in good faith.

5. Po.O duty: Po.O, Prt. O, SP or Mag. receives DV complaint/otherwise present at DV incident place/when DV incident report him inform Agg. P her right to Appl. for relief by PO, monetary relief, custody/residence/ compensate order; SP's & Prt.O service available; free legal services under LSAA; complaint u/s 498A IPC, if relevant file. Not relieve Po.O his duty to

proceed in law on cognizable offence commit.

6. SH Duty: If Agg. P/ her behalf Prt. O/ SP request SH in charge, provide SH shelter.

7. MF Duty: If Agg. P/ her behalf Prt. O/ SP request MF in charge provide any MA to her, such person provide it.

8. Prt. O appoint: CG notify for each district & areas exercise powers & duty, women preferable & qualifications & experience, service terms & conditions & other officers subordinate be such AMBP.

9. Prt.O Duty: assist Mag.; make DIR to Mag. upon DV complaint receipt & copy to Po.O in charge of Po.S WTLL whose Jur. DV alleged commit & area SPs; Appl. AMBP to Mag., if Agg. P so desire, claim relief for PO issue; provide legal aid under LSAA & PF free of cost complaint made; maintain all SPs list providing legal aid/cou., SHs & MF in Mag. Jur.; make safe SH, if Agg. P require & forward his report to Po.S & Mag. Jur. of SH; get Agg. P ME, if bodily injury & forward Po.S MR copy & to Mag. Jur. where DV alleged; ensure monetary relief u/s 20 order comply & execute under Cr. PC; other duties AMBP, under Mag. control & supervise & Govt.

10. SP: any VA in SRA/CA/law in force object to protect women rights & interest by any lawful means include legal aid, medical, financial, etc. assist register with CG as SP for PTA. SP power to record DIR in PF if Agg. P so desire & forward copy to Mag. & Prt. O Jur. where DV took place; get Agg. P ME & forward MR copy to Prt. O & Po.S WTLL of which DV took place; Agg. P provided shelter in SH, if require & forward report to lodge to Po.S WTLL of which DV took place. No suit, etc. against any SP/member deem act/purport UTA, in good faith in exercise of power/discharge functions UTA towards prevent to CV commit.

CHAPTER IV: PROCEDURE FOR OBTAINING ORDERS OF RELIEF

12. Appl. to Mag.: An Agg. P/Prt. O/behalf of Agg. P present Appl. to Mag. seeks relief. Mag. consider DIR receive from Prt. O/SP. Relief include compensate/damages pay w/o prejudice to right of such person institute injury suit for DV commit by Resp. Decree by Court in Agg. P favour for amount, paid/payable under Mag. order set off against under such decree & NWAC CPC/any other law executable for balance amount left after set off. Every Appl. such form, particulars AMBP/ possible thereto. Mag. fix 1st DOH, not beyond 3 D from its receipt by court & dispose in next 60 D.

13. Notice serve: Hearing fixed u/s 12 by Mag. to Prt. O serve such means AMBP on Resp. & other person, as Mag. direct in 2 D/such further as he allow. Declaration of Service be proof serve as direct, unless contrary

proved.

14. Cou.: Mag. any stage of proceeding direct Resp./Agg. P undergo cou. with any SP member possess such qualifications & experience AMBP & fix NDOH not beyond 2 M.

15. Welfare Expert: In any proceeding, Mag. may secure services, preferably woman, related/not to Agg. P, include those promote family welfare to assist his functions discharge.

16. Proceedings in camera: if Mag. considers so warrant & if either party desire conduct in camera.

17. Right to reside in a shared household: NWAC other law every woman in DR right to reside in shared household, whether/not any right, title, etc. in it. Not evict/exclude from it by Resp. save under law process.

18. PO: Mag. after Agg. P & Resp. hearing opportunity & prima facie satisfy that DV taken/likely, pass PO in favour of Agg. P & prohibit Resp. from DV commit; aid/abet DV; enter employment place of Agg. P/if Agg. P child, its school/place frequented by her; communicate with Agg. P; alienate assets, operate bank account, etc. both parties, jointly/singly by Resp., include her stridhan/property held w/o Mag. leave; cause violence to dependent/ relatives, etc. who give Agg. P assistance from DV; commit any other act PO specify.

19. Residence order: While disposing Appl. u/s 12(1) Mag. satisfy DV taken place, pass order restrain Resp. from dispossess/disturb Agg. P from shared household, whether/not Resp. has legal/equitable interest in shared household; direct Resp. to remove himself from shared household, however, no such order against woman; restrain Resp./relatives enter any portion of shared household in which Agg. P reside; restrain Resp. alienate/dispose shared household; restrain Resp. renounce rights in shared household except Mag. leave; direct Resp. secure alternate accommodation for Agg. P as enjoyed in shared household/pay rent if require. Mag. may impose additional conditions, etc. necessary for Agg. P/her child safety. Require Resp. execute bond, with or w/o surety, to prevent DV commit, deem order under Chapter VIII Cr. PC & dealt accordingly. Also pass order direct nearest Po.S in charge protect Agg. P/assist Appl. implement order. Mag. imposes on Resp. obligation to discharge rent & other financial need & resources of parties. Mag. may direct officer in-charge of Po.S in whose Jur. Mag. approach assist PO implement & direct Resp. possession return of Agg. P her stridhan/property/valuable security, etc. entitled.

20. Monetary relief: While dispose Appl. u/s 12(1), Mag. may direct Resp. pay relief expenses incur & loss suffered by Agg. P & its child due to DV & not limit to loss of earnings; medical expenses; property under Agg. P control destruction & her maintenance & children, include maintenance u/s 125 Cr. PC/law in force. Relief be adequate, fair & reasonable & consistent with living standard Agg. P accustom. Order lump sum payment/monthly payment, as circumstance requires. Mag. send order copy to parties to Appl. & in charge of Po.S WTLL of whose Jur. Resp. reside who pay to Agg. P in period, if fails, Mag. direct employer/Resp. debtor, directly pay to Agg. P/ deposit in court a portion of wages/salary/debt due/accrued to credit of Resp., be adjusted towards monetary relief payable by Resp.

21. Custody: NWAC other law, Mag. any stage hear of Appl. for PO/any other relief UTA grant temporary custody of children to Agg. P/person make Appl. & arrange visit by Resp., Mag. refuse if opine harmful to children interest.

22. Compensate: In addition to other relief, Mag. on Appl. by Agg. P, direct Resp. pay compensation & damage for injury, mental torture & emotional distress.

23. Interim & exparte order: Mag. order just & proper satisfy Appl. prima facie disclose Resp. is committing/committed DV act/likelihood commit, ex parte order on Affidavit, AMBP of Agg. P u/s 18-22 against Resp.

24. Order copy: Mag. pass order, copy free of cost to Parties to Appl., Po.O in-charge of Po.S in Jur. & SP located WTLL of Jur. of Court & to any SP register DIR.

25. Orders duration & alter: PO u/s 18 in force till Agg. P apply for discharge & Mag. on receipt satisfy circumstance requires to alter, etc. any order, reasons record pass appropriate order.

26. Relief: u/s 18-22 relief also seek in civil/family/criminal court, affect Agg. P & Resp., in addition to & other relief, if taken, inform Mag.

27. Jur.: 1st class JM/MM, WTLL Agg. P/Resp. resides/business carry/ employed/cause of action arose competent court to grant PO & other orders & offence try & any order enforceable throughout India.

28. Procedure: All proceedings u/s 12, 18-23 & offence u/s 31 Cr. PC governs. Not prevent Court lay own procedure Appl. u/s 12/23(2) dispose.

29. Appeal: COS in 30 D from date Mag. order serve on Agg. P/Resp.

CHAPTER V: MISCELLANEOUS

30. Prt. O & SP member's public servant: acts/purport to act under Pr. A/ rules/orders public servant u/s 21 IPC.

31. PO Breach by Resp.: PO/interim PO breach is offence & upto 1 Yr Jail/Rs.20K Fine/Both. Mag. try passed order, breach by accused. While he frames charges, also u/s 498A IPC/ that Code/ DPA, if facts disclose offence commit therein.

32. Cognizance & proof: NWAC Cr. PC, offence u/s 31 cognizable & no-bail, upon sole testimony of Agg. P, Court conclude Accused commit.

33. Penalty: If Prt. O fails/not discharge duty Mag. Direct in PO w/o cause, upto 1 Yr Jail/ Rs.2,000 fine/Both.

34. Cognizance: No prosecution, etc. against Prt. O unless CG previous sanction complaint/officer authorized.

35. Protect act in good faith: No suit, prosecution, etc. against Prt. O on damage caused/likely done/intended.

36. Act not in derogation other law: Pr. A is in addition.

ABBREVIATIONS

1st- First

1 Y- One Year

2,000- Two Thousand

20 K- Twenty Thousand

2 D- Two Days

3 D- Three Days

30 D- Thirty Days

60 D- Sixty Days

2 M- Two Months

&- And

Agg. P- Aggrieved Person

AMBP- As may be Prescribed

Appl. – Application

CA- Companies Act, 1956

CG- Central Government

Cou.- Counseling COS- Court of Session

CPC- Code of Civil Procedure, 1908

Cr. PC- Code of Criminal Procedure, 1973 DIR- Domestic Incident Report

DOH- Date of Hearing

DPA- Dowry Prohibition Act, 1961

DR- Domestic Relationship

DV- Domestic Violence

Expl- Explanation

IPC - Indian Penal Code, 1860

Jur. - Jurisdiction

JM- Judicial Magistrate

LSAA- Legal Services Authorities Act, 1987

Mag. – Magistrate

MA- Medical Aid

ME- Medical Examine

MF- Medical Facility/ies

MR- Medical Report

NDOH- Next Date of Hearing

MM- Metropolitan Magistrate

NWAC- Notwithstanding anything contained in

PF- Prescribed Form
PO- Protection Order/s
Po. O- Police Officer
Po.S- Police Station
Pr. A- Provisions of this Act
Prt. O - Protection Officer/s
PTA- Purposes of this Act
Resp. – Respondent
SG- State Government
SH- Shelter Home/s
SP- Service Provider
SRA- Societies Registration Act, 1860
U/S – Under Section
UTA- Under this Act
VA- Voluntary Association
W/o- Without
WTLL- Within Local Limits
Yrs - Years